ENCHANTING ORIGAMI

Fantastic Food ORIGAMI

JOE FULLMAN

WINDMILL BOOKS

Published in 2021 by Windmill Books,
an Imprint of Rosen Publishing
29 East 21st Street, New York, NY 10010

Cataloging-in-Publication Data

Names: Fullman, Joe.
Title: Fantastic food origami / Joe Fullman.
Description: New York : Windmill Books, 2021. | Series: Enchanting origami | Includes glossary and index.
Identifiers: ISBN 9781499485332 (pbk.) | ISBN 9781499485356 (library bound) | ISBN 9781499485349 (6 pack) | ISBN 9781499485363 (ebook)
Subjects: LCSH: Origami--Juvenile literature. | Food in art--Juvenile literature.
Classification: LCC TT872.5 F85 2021 | DDC 736'.982--dc23

Manufactured in the United States of America

CPSIA Compliance Information: Batch BS20WM: For Further Information contact Rosen Publishing, New York, New York at 1-800-237-9932

Contents

Introduction

Let's explore the wonderful world of enchanted origami. In this book, we'll enjoy a tasty picnic, including ice-cream cones, slices of watermelon, juicy strawberries, and pretty cupcakes.

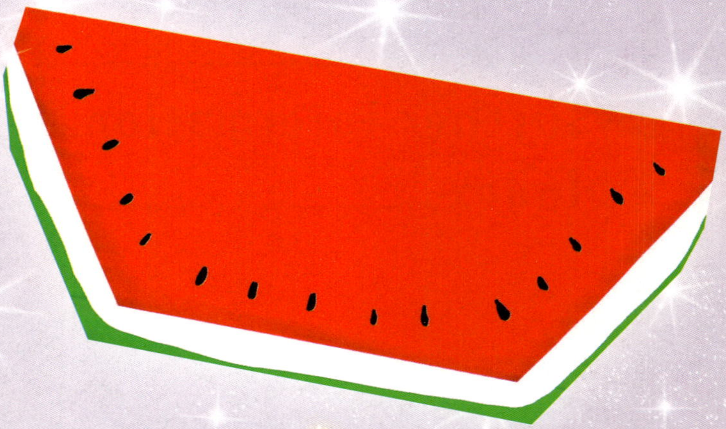

In traditional origami, the models are usually made from a single sheet of folded paper with no cutting or gluing involved. We've broken the rules here and there to make our models as magical as possible.

Ask an adult to help with any projects that need scissors and glue. Otherwise, all you need to get started is a square of paper and your fingers. If you haven't made origami models before, try some of the easy projects first. Now, let's get ready for some fantastic folding!

Getting Started

The paper used in origami is thin but strong, so that it can be folded many times. You can use ordinary scrap paper, as long as it's not too thick.

A lot of these origami models are made with the same folds and basic starting designs, known as "bases." This introduction explains some of the ones that will appear most, so it's a good idea to master these before you start. When making the projects, follow the key to find out what the lines and arrows mean. And always crease well!

Key

- Valley fold
- Mountain fold
- Step fold
- Direction to move paper
- Push/flatten
- Rotate by x degrees
- Cut with scissors
- Glue
- Turn paper over

Basic Folds

Valley Fold

To make a valley fold, fold the edges of the paper toward you, so that the crease is pointing down, like a valley.

Mountain Fold

To make a mountain fold, fold the edges of the paper away from you, so that the crease is pointing up, like a mountain.

Step Fold

A step fold is used to make a step or zigzag in the paper.

1

Valley fold the paper in half. Then make a mountain fold directly above the valley fold.

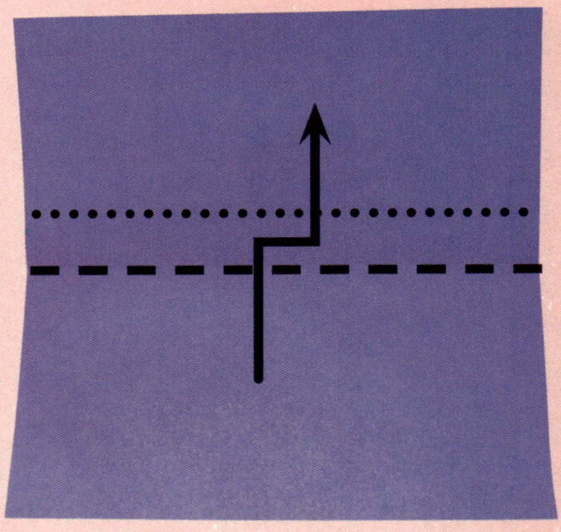

2

Push the mountain fold over the valley fold and press down flat.

3

You now have a step fold. You can also make it in reverse, with the mountain fold first.

Kite Base

1

Place your paper like this. Valley fold it in half from left to right.

2

Valley fold the left-hand point over to the middle crease.

3

Repeat step 2 on the other side.

4

You now have a kite base.

Ice Cream

Time to cool off with a delicious ice-cream cone. Make several so everyone can have one of their own.

1

Start with a kite base (see page 7) positioned like this. Make a diagonal valley fold in the upper layer on the right-hand side to create a new triangle-shaped flap.

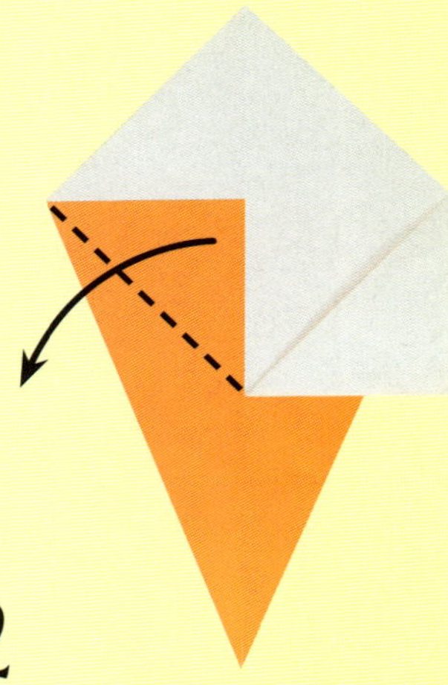

2

Make a diagonal valley fold in the upper layer on the left-hand side so it matches the flap made in step 1.

3

Mountain fold the right-hand point behind the paper.

4

Repeat step 3 on the left-hand side.

5

Turn the paper over from left to right.

6

Valley fold the top-right edge over to the central crease. The new flap will go over the flap you made in step 3.

Easy

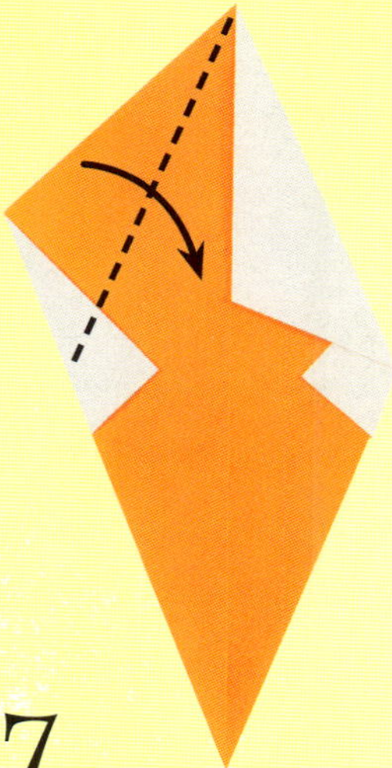

7

Repeat step 6 on the left-hand side.

8

Your paper should look like this. Make a step fold in the top half (see page 6) with the valley fold below the mountain fold.

9

Push the paper down flat.

10

Turn the paper over from left to right.

11

Make another step fold closer to the top point, but this time with the mountain fold line below the valley fold line.

12

Push the paper down flat.

13

You could add some glittery sprinkles to the top of your ice-cream cone. Then you'd better give it to a unicorn to eat before it melts!

Watermelon

Here's a healthy alternative to ice cream—a slice of watermelon. It's just as refreshing on a hot summer day.

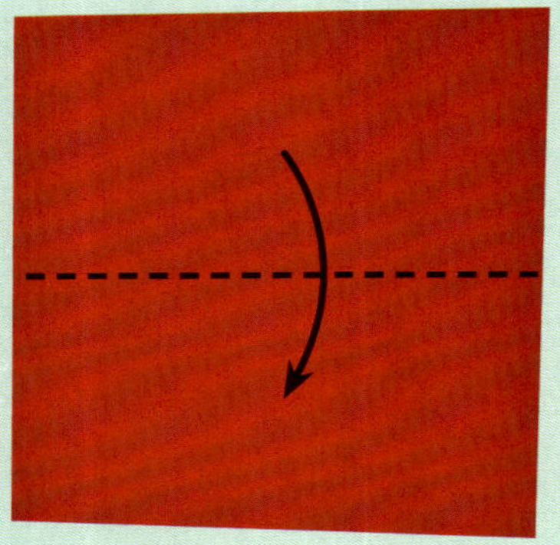

1

Place your paper like this, white side down, with a straight edge facing you. Valley fold in half from top to bottom, and then unfold.

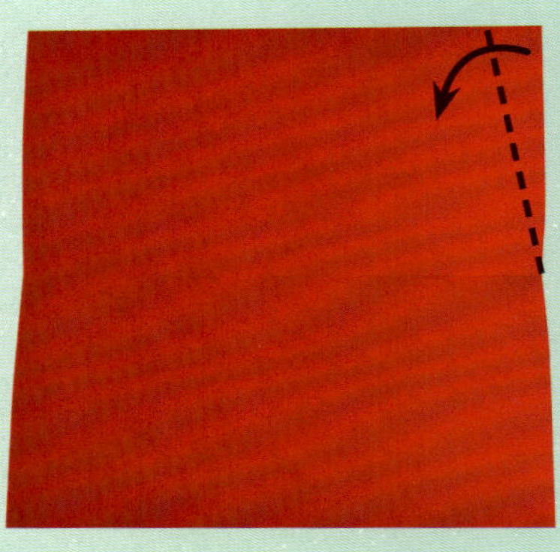

2

Make a small diagonal valley fold in the top right corner, as shown.

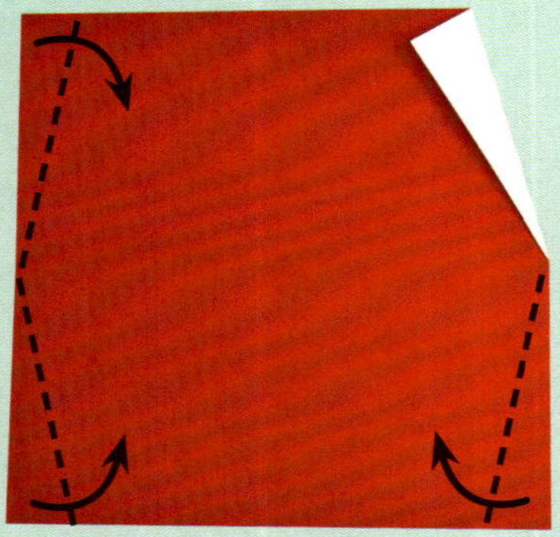

3

Repeat step 2 with the other three corners.

4

Valley fold over the top edge, as shown.

5

Repeat step 4 on the bottom edge.

Easy

6
Mountain fold the top right corner, as shown.

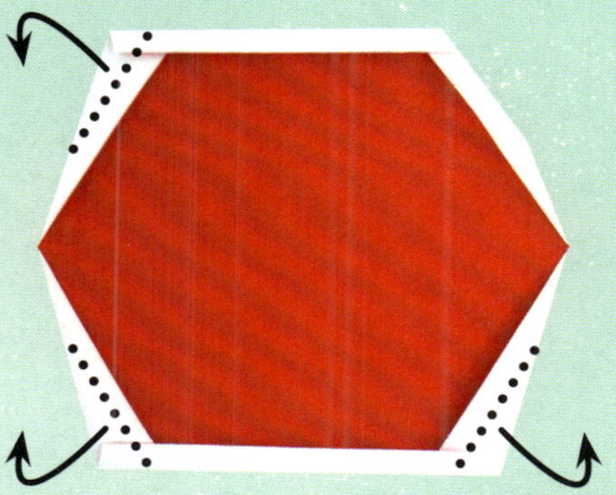

7
Repeat step 6 with the top left, bottom left, and bottom right corners.

8
Mountain fold the right-hand point, as shown.

9
Mountain fold the left-hand point.

10
Mountain fold the paper in half from top to bottom

11
And there's a tasty slice of watermelon. Use a green marker to draw the rind, and then add some seeds. Delicious!

Popsicle

Follow these instructions to make a tasty frozen snack. Be sure to hold it by the stick so your hands don't get too cold! You'll need scissors for this project.

1

Start with your paper like this, white side down, with a straight edge facing you. Valley fold in half from left to right, and then unfold.

2

Use scissors to carefully cut your paper in half along the crease line you made in step 1.

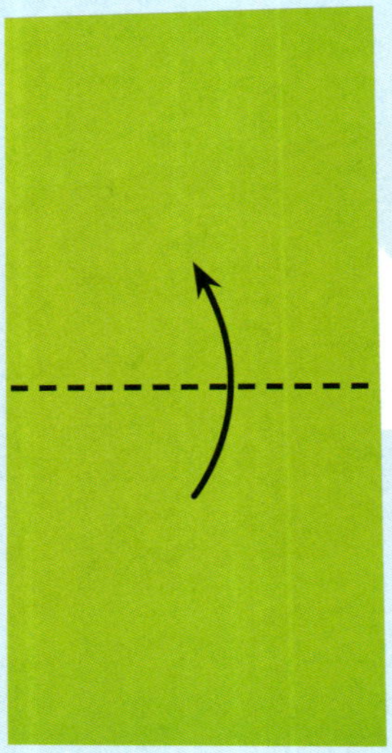

3

Take one of the pieces of paper and valley fold it in half from bottom to top.

4

Unfold the fold you made in step 3.

Medium

5

Valley fold the bottom edge up to the central crease.

6

Turn the paper over from left to right.

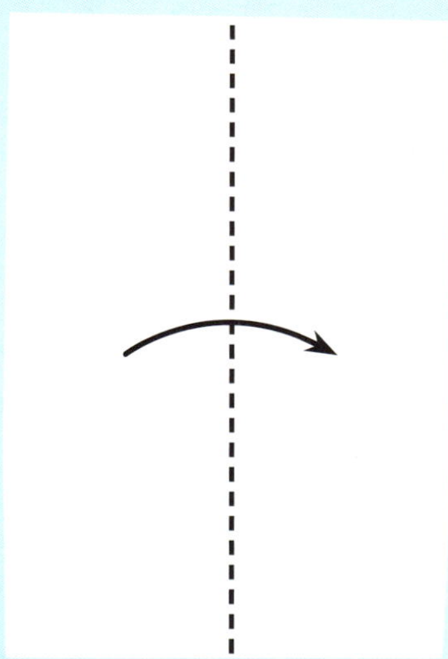

7

Fold the paper in half from left to right.

8

Unfold the fold you made in step 7.

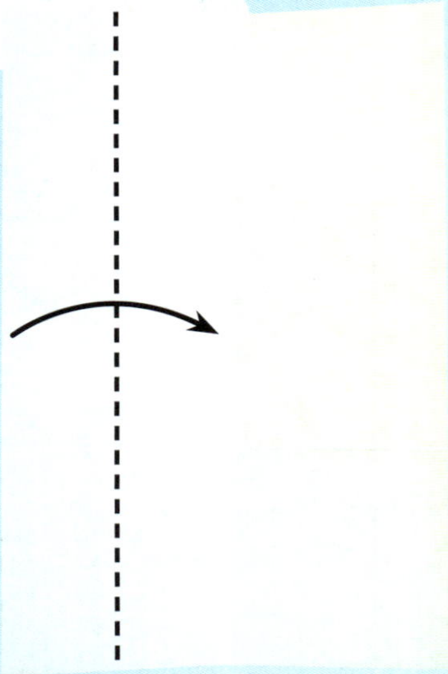

9

Fold the left-hand edge over to the central crease.

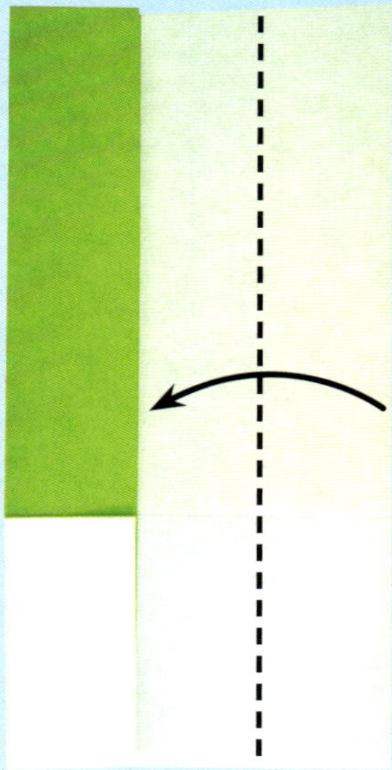

10

Fold the right-hand edge over to the central crease.

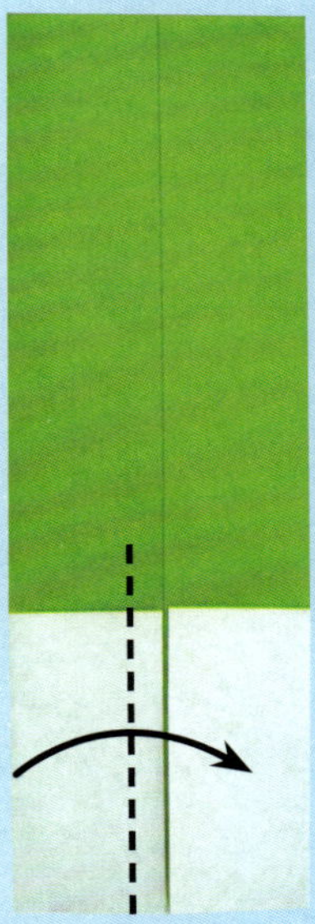

11

Make a valley fold, as shown, around three-quarters of the way between the left-hand edge and the central line. Don't crease all the way along the paper, just from the bottom edge to slightly above the white area.

12

Crease well, then unfold.

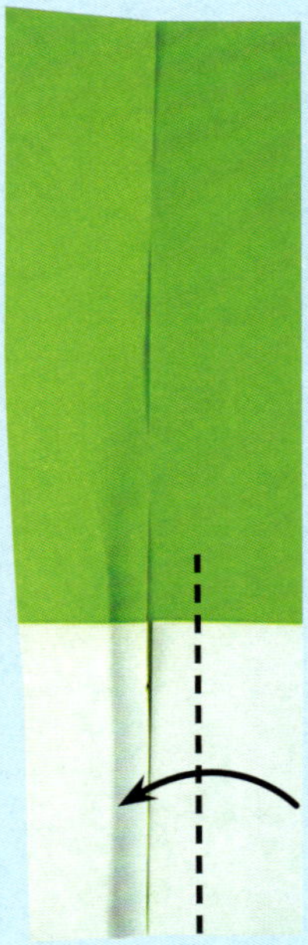

13

Make a similar fold on the right-hand side, but this time around two-thirds of the way between the right-hand edge and the central line, so that, when you fold it, the edge lines up with the crease you made in step 12.

14

Again, don't crease it all the way, just from the bottom edge to just above the white area. Unfold.

Medium

TURN OVER

15

Your paper should look like this. Turn it over from left to right.

16

Valley fold the bottom edge up. Make the crease at the top of the white area.

17

Make a small diagonal valley fold in the bottom corner, as shown, in line with the crease you made in step 11.

18

Repeat step 17 on the left-hand side. Make the crease just slightly farther over than the crease line from step 13, so it matches the fold in step 17.

TURN OVER

19

Turn your paper over from left to right.

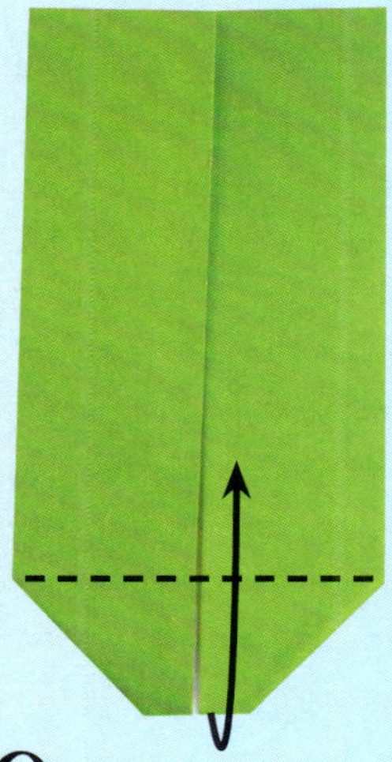

20

Make a horizontal valley fold at the bottom of the paper, as shown. Flip the lower layer forward so the white area appears again at the bottom of the paper.

21

Your paper should look like this. Unfold the folds you made in steps 17 and 18.

22

Open out the white area at the top on the right-hand side.

23

Push the top right point down and to the left so it forms a triangle shape. This should make the paper fold over along the line of the fold you made in step 13.

24

Flatten the triangle shape down.

25

Your paper should look like this. Repeat steps 22 and 23 on the left-hand side.

26

Flatten the triangle shape down.

Medium

27

Valley fold the top right point, as shown.

28

Repeat step 27 on the left-hand side.

29

Turn your paper over from left to right.

30

That's one popsicle done. Make sure you make enough for everyone!

Strawberry

Here's how to make an origami strawberry, the perfect summer fruit. All magical (and non-magical) creatures love them!

1
Place your paper like this, white side up, with a corner facing you. Valley fold it in half from top to bottom.

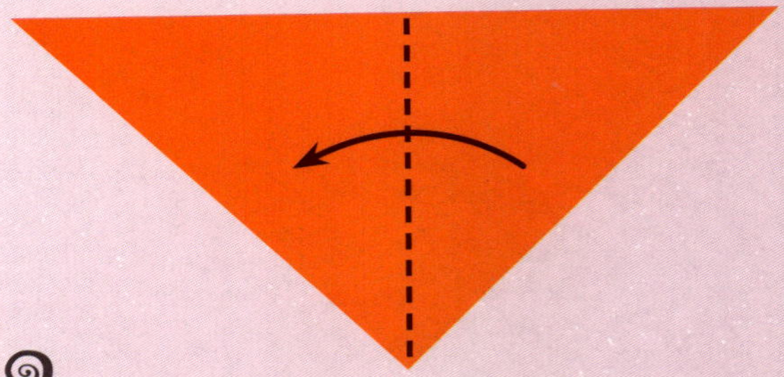

2
Valley fold the paper in half from right to left.

3
Unfold the fold you made in step 2.

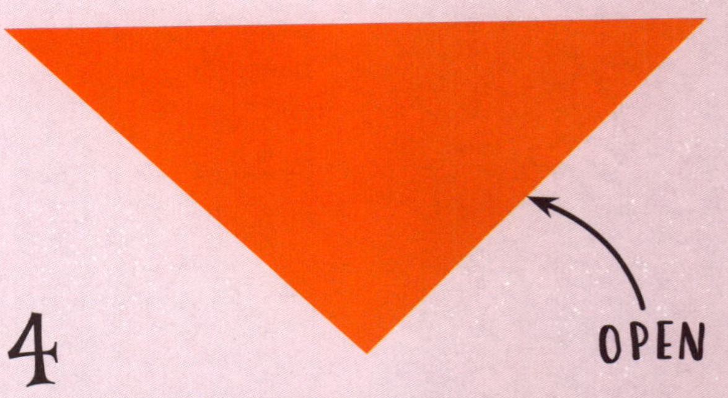

4
Open up the paper on the right-hand side, so it forms a shape a bit like a bird's mouth.

Easy

5

Bring the top right point down to the bottom point. Flatten the paper down.

6

Your paper should look like this. Turn it over from left to right.

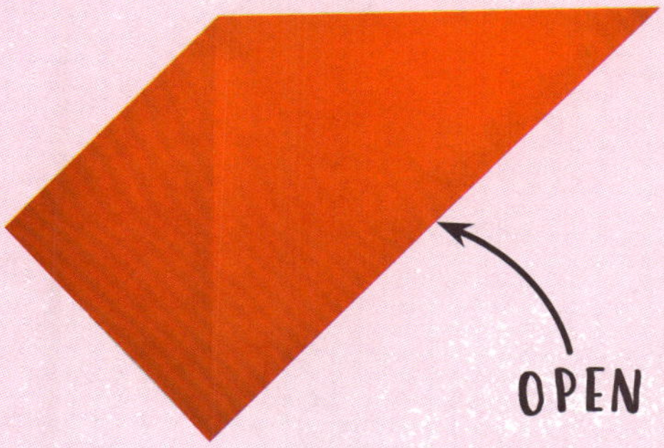

7

Open up the paper on the right-hand side.

8

Repeat step 5, bringing the top right point down to the bottom point, then flattening the paper.

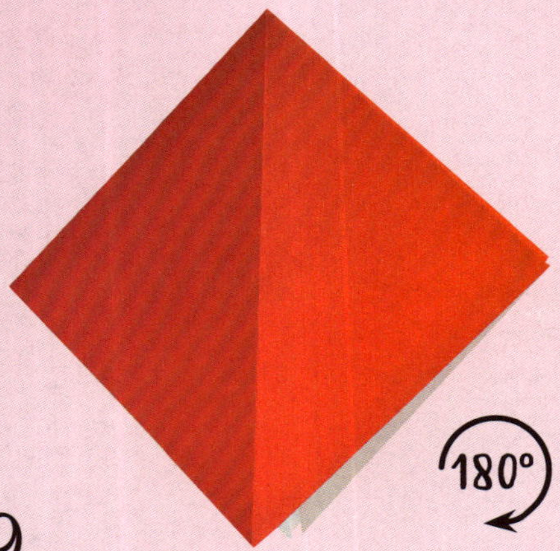

9
Rotate your paper 180°, so the open points are at the top.

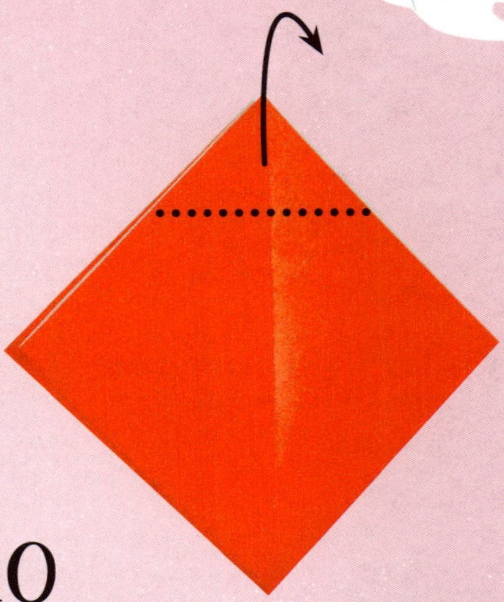

10
Mountain fold the top point of the upper layer, as shown.

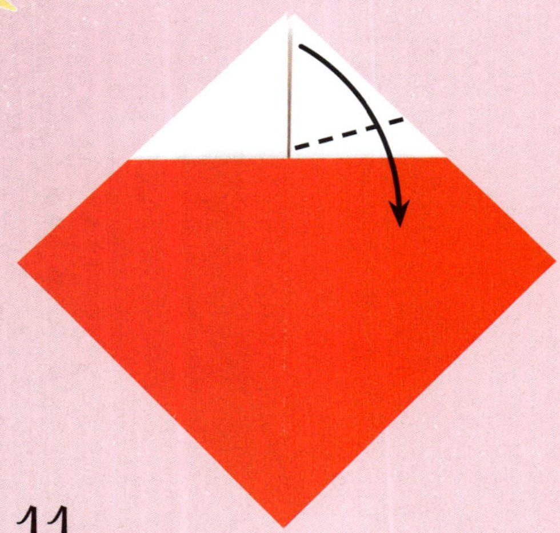

11
Valley fold the top point of the new upper layer down and to the right, as shown.

12
Repeat step 11 on the left-hand side.

Easy

13

Make a mountain fold on the right-hand side, as shown. Crease well.

14

Repeat step 13 on the left-hand side.

15

Valley fold over the top point.

16

Add some seeds, decorate the leaves, and your strawberry is ready. It looks good enough to eat!

Cupcake

No picnic is complete without cupcakes! Get lots of sheets of paper so you can make all different kinds!

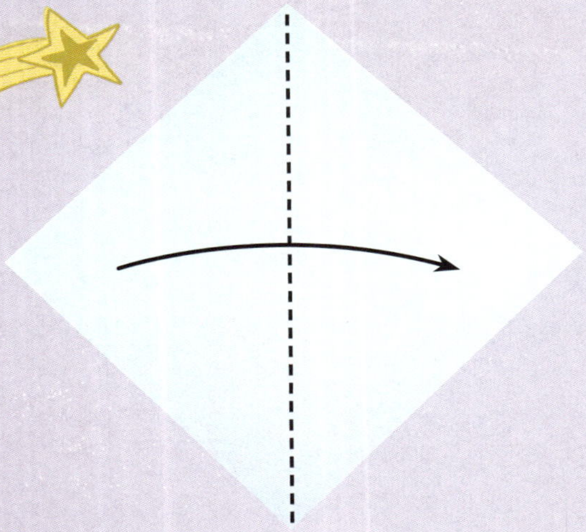

1 Place your paper like this, white side up, with a corner facing you. Valley fold in half from left to right, then unfold.

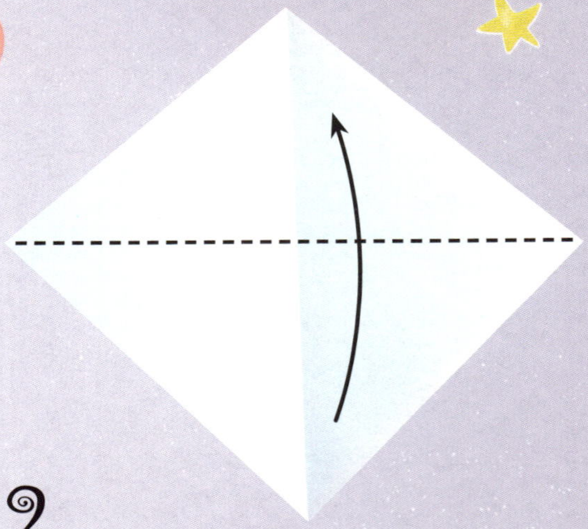

2 Valley fold your paper in half from bottom to top.

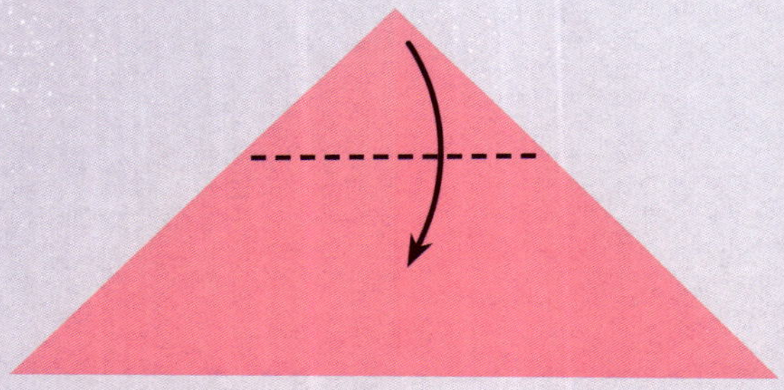

3 Valley fold the top point of the upper layer about a third of the way from the top.

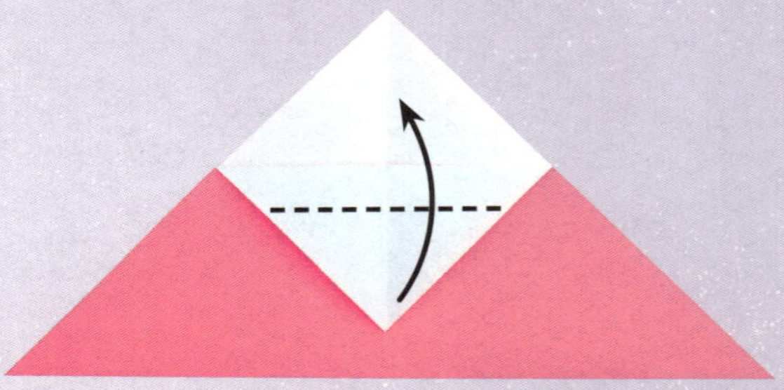

4 Valley fold the point up again, as shown.

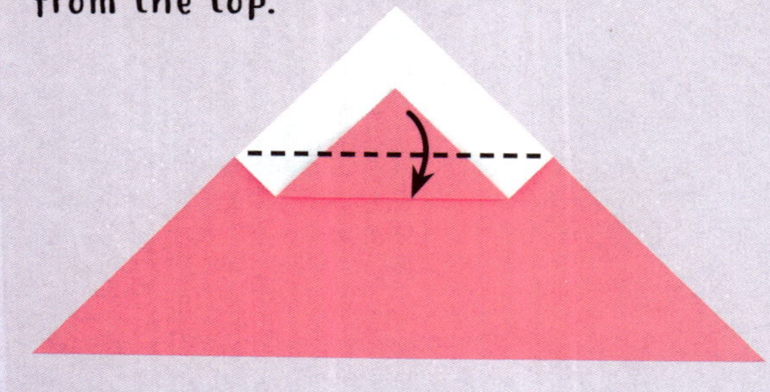

5 Valley fold the point again, in line with the crease you made in step 3.

6 Valley fold the point one more time in line with the crease you made in step 4.

Easy

7 Make a step fold at the top of the paper (see page 6), with the mountain fold below the valley fold.

8 Flatten the paper down.

9 Valley fold the top point over the layer above it, as shown.

10 Mountain fold the right-hand side at an angle.

11 Repeat step 10 on the left-hand side.

12

That's your first cupcake baked! Add some glittery sprinkles to the top. Delicious!

Glossary

CREASE A line made by a fold.

DIAGONAL A line in a sloping direction, from one corner to another.

KITE BASE A starting shape that looks like a kite.

MOUNTAIN FOLD A fold where the crease points up, like a mountain.

STEP FOLD A fold that creates a zigzag, or step, in the paper.

VALLEY FOLD A fold where the crease points away from you, like a valley.

Further Information

James, Elizabeth. *Easy Origami for Children*. Twickenham, UK: Kyle Craig Publishing, 2017.

Montroll, John. *Dragons and Other Fantastic Creatures in Origami*. Mineola, NY: Dover Publications, 2014.

Stephen, Ella. *Origami for Kids*. Independently published, 2019.

Top That Publishing. *Fold Your Own Fantastic Fairytale Unicorns*. Woodbridge, UK: Top That Publishing, 2019.

Index